THIS JOURNAL BELONGS TO:

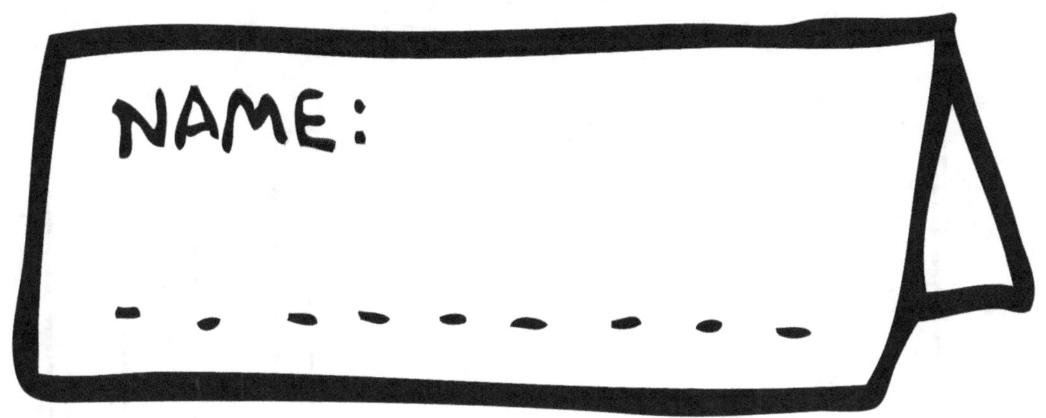

NEWSPAPER

TUESDAY

THURSDAY

SAT/SUN

MONDAY

WEDNESDAY

FRIDAY

NEWSPAPER

MONDAY

TUESDAY

WEDNESDAY

THURSDAY

FRIDAY

SAT/SUN

SAT/SUN

NEWSPAPER

MONDAY

TUESDAY

WEDNESDAY

THURSDAY

FRIDAY

SAT/SUN

NEWSPAPER

MONDAY
TUESDAY
WEDNESDAY
THURSDAY
FRIDAY
SAT/SUN

SAT/SUN

NEWSPAPER

MONDAY TUESDAY WEDNESDAY THURSDAY FRIDAY SAT/SUN

NEWSPAPER

MONDAY

TUESDAY

WEDNESDAY

THURSDAY

FRIDAY

SAT/SUN

NEWSPAPER

MONDAY

TUESDAY

WEDNESDAY

THURSDAY

FRIDAY

SAT/SUN

NEWSPAPER

TUESDAY

THURSDAY

SAT/SUN

MONDAY

WEDNESDAY

FRIDAY

SAT/SUN

NEWSPAPER
PHOTO HERE
STORY BODY

MONDAY
TUESDAY
WEDNESDAY
THURSDAY
FRIDAY
SAT/SUN

SAT/SUN

NEWSPAPER

MONDAY
TUESDAY
WEDNESDAY
THURSDAY
FRIDAY
SAT/SUN

NEWSPAPER

TUESDAY

THURSDAY

SAT/SUN

MONDAY

WEDNESDAY

FRIDAY

NEWSPAPER

MONDAY

TUESDAY

WEDNESDAY

THURSDAY

FRIDAY

SAT/SUN

NEWSPAPER
(DATE TAKEN)
(STORY BODY)

TUESDAY

THURSDAY

SAT/SUN

MONDAY

WEDNESDAY

FRIDAY

SAT/SUN

NEWSPAPER

MONDAY
TUESDAY
WEDNESDAY
THURSDAY
FRIDAY
SAT/SUN

NEWSPAPER

MONDAY

TUESDAY

WEDNESDAY

THURSDAY

FRIDAY

SAT/SUN

NEWSPAPER

MONDAY

TUESDAY

WEDNESDAY

THURSDAY

FRIDAY

SAT/SUN

SAT/SUN

NEWSPAPER

MONDAY
TUESDAY
WEDNESDAY
THURSDAY
FRIDAY
SAT/SUN

NEWSPAPER

TUESDAY

THURSDAY

SAT/SUN

MONDAY

WEDNESDAY

FRIDAY

SAT/SUN

NEWSPAPER

MONDAY
TUESDAY
WEDNESDAY
THURSDAY
FRIDAY
SAT/SUN

NEWSPAPER

MONDAY TUESDAY

WEDNESDAY THURSDAY

FRIDAY SAT/SUN

NEWSPAPER

MONDAY
TUESDAY
WEDNESDAY
THURSDAY
FRIDAY
SAT/SUN

SAT/SUN

NEWSPAPER

MONDAY

TUESDAY

WEDNESDAY

THURSDAY

FRIDAY

SAT/SUN

NEWSPAPER
(NAME OF PAPER)
(STORY HEADLINE)
(DRAW PICTURE OF STORY)
(DATE TAKEN)
(PHOTO TAKEN)
(STORY BODY)
(STORY TEXT)

MONDAY TUESDAY

WEDNESDAY THURSDAY

FRIDAY SAT/SUN

SAT/SUN

NEWSPAPER

MONDAY	TUESDAY
WEDNESDAY	THURSDAY
FRIDAY	SAT/SUN

SAT/SUN

NEWSPAPER

MONDAY TUESDAY
WEDNESDAY THURSDAY
FRIDAY SAT/SUN

SAT/SUN

NEWSPAPER

MONDAY

TUESDAY

WEDNESDAY

THURSDAY

FRIDAY

SAT/SUN

NEWSPAPER

MONDAY

TUESDAY

WEDNESDAY

THURSDAY

FRIDAY

SAT/SUN

NEWSPAPER

TUESDAY
THURSDAY
SAT/SUN
MONDAY
WEDNESDAY
FRIDAY

SAT/SUN

NEWSPAPER

TUESDAY

THURSDAY

SAT/SUN

MONDAY

WEDNESDAY

FRIDAY

NEWSPAPER

MONDAY
TUESDAY
WEDNESDAY
THURSDAY
FRIDAY
SAT/SUN

NEWSPAPER

MONDAY

TUESDAY

WEDNESDAY

THURSDAY

FRIDAY

SAT/SUN

NEWSPAPER

MONDAY

TUESDAY

WEDNESDAY

THURSDAY

FRIDAY

SAT/SUN

NEWSPAPER
(NAME OF PAPER)
(STORY HEADLINE)
(MAIN PICTURE OF STORY)
(DATE TAKEN)
(PHOTO CREDIT)
(STORY BODY)

MONDAY

TUESDAY

WEDNESDAY

THURSDAY

FRIDAY

SAT/SUN

NEWSPAPER

MONDAY
TUESDAY
WEDNESDAY
THURSDAY
FRIDAY
SAT/SUN

NEWSPAPER

MONDAY

TUESDAY

WEDNESDAY

THURSDAY

FRIDAY

SAT/SUN

SAT/SUN

NEWSPAPER

MONDAY

TUESDAY

WEDNESDAY

THURSDAY

FRIDAY

SAT/SUN

SAT/SUN

NEWSPAPER

MONDAY	TUESDAY
WEDNESDAY	THURSDAY
FRIDAY	SAT/SUN

NEWSPAPER

MONDAY
TUESDAY
WEDNESDAY
THURSDAY
FRIDAY
SAT/SUN

NEWSPAPER

MONDAY   TUESDAY

WEDNESDAY   THURSDAY

FRIDAY   SAT/SUN

NEWSPAPER

MONDAY

TUESDAY

WEDNESDAY

THURSDAY

FRIDAY

SAT/SUN

SAT/SUN

NEWSPAPER

MONDAY

TUESDAY

WEDNESDAY

THURSDAY

FRIDAY

SAT/SUN

NEWSPAPER

MONDAY

TUESDAY

WEDNESDAY

THURSDAY

FRIDAY

SAT/SUN

NEWSPAPER
(NAME OF PAPER)
(STORY HEADLINE)
(DRAW PICTURE OF STORY)
(DATE TAKEN)
(PHOTO USED)
(STORY BODY)
(STORY TEXT)
(DRAW OTHER PICTURE)
(STORY TEXT)

MONDAY

TUESDAY

WEDNESDAY

THURSDAY

FRIDAY

SAT/SUN

NEWSPAPER

MONDAY TUESDAY WEDNESDAY THURSDAY FRIDAY SAT/SUN

SAT/SUN

NEWSPAPER

MONDAY

TUESDAY

WEDNESDAY

THURSDAY

FRIDAY

SAT/SUN

NEWSPAPER

MONDAY
TUESDAY
WEDNESDAY
THURSDAY
FRIDAY
SAT/SUN

NEWSPAPER

MONDAY	TUESDAY	
WEDNESDAY	THURSDAY	
FRIDAY		SAT/SUN

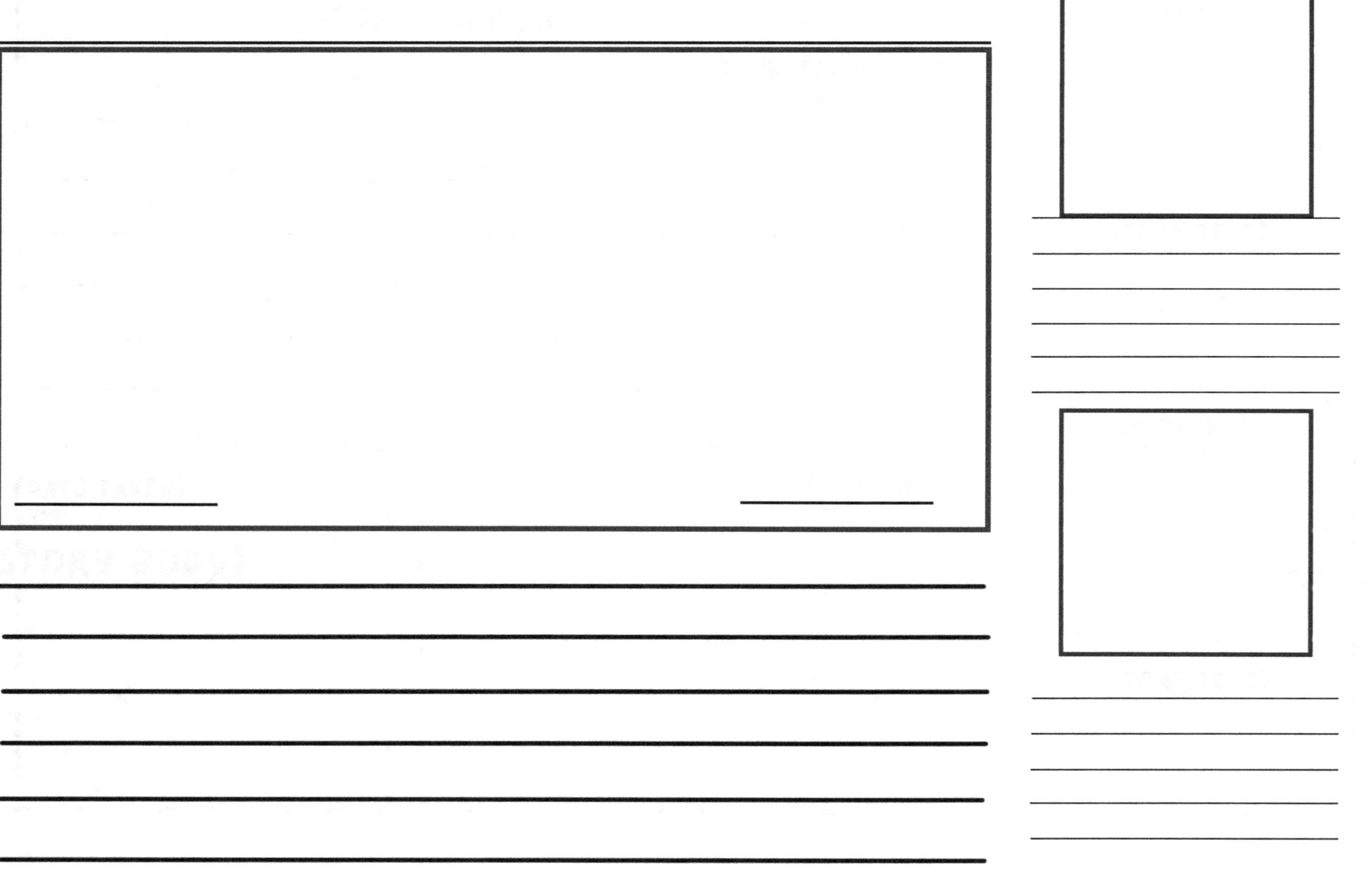
NEWSPAPER
(PICTURE)
(STORY BODY)

MONDAY TUESDAY

WEDNESDAY THURSDAY

FRIDAY SAT/SUN

SAT/SUN

NEWSPAPER

MONDAY

TUESDAY

WEDNESDAY

THURSDAY

FRIDAY

SAT/SUN

SAT/SUN

NEWSPAPER

MONDAY

TUESDAY

WEDNESDAY

THURSDAY

FRIDAY

SAT/SUN

SAT/SUN

NEWSPAPER

MONDAY

TUESDAY

WEDNESDAY

THURSDAY

FRIDAY

SAT/SUN

NEWSPAPER

MONDAY

TUESDAY

WEDNESDAY

THURSDAY

FRIDAY

SAT/SUN

SAT/SUN

NEWSPAPER

MONDAY

TUESDAY

WEDNESDAY

THURSDAY

FRIDAY

SAT/SUN

SAT/SUN

NEWSPAPER

MONDAY
TUESDAY
WEDNESDAY
THURSDAY
FRIDAY
SAT/SUN

NEWSPAPER LINGO

- CLASSIFIED ADS: A SECTION PURCHASED TO SELL OR ANNOUNCE INFORMATION ON A BUDGET.
- NEWS ARTICLE/STORY: A REPORT ON AN EVENT THAT HAS TAKEN PLACE.

- EDITOR: DECIDES WHAT WILL BE INCLUDED IN THE PAPER AND WHERE.
- ADVERTISEMENTS: A SECTION PURCHASED FOR SELLING A PRODUCT OR IDEA.
- EDITORIAL CARTOONS OR COMIC: USED TO CONVEY A MESSAGE USING HUMOR OR VISUAL DESCRIPTION.
- PHOTO CREDIT: WHO TOOK THE PHOTOGRAPH.

- HEADLINE: A SENSATIONAL OR IMPORTANT NEWS PIECE.
- MINOR STORY: A STORY NOT AS SENSATIONAL AS THE HEADLINE BUT STILL WORTH REPORTING ON.

www.ingramcontent.com/pod-product-compliance
Lightning Source LLC
Chambersburg PA
CBHW081929120726
47997CB00010B/3097